OH GOD, WOULD YOU REND THE HEAVENS?

UNDERSTANDING AND CONTENDING FOR A
GENUINE SPIRITUAL AWAKENING

SHANE IDLEMAN

EL PASEO PUBLICATIONS

Oh God, Would You Rend the Heavens?

Understanding and Contending for a Genuine Spiritual Awakening

Published by El Paseo Publications

Printed in the United States of America

Interior design by Steve Bremner and initial editing by Christine Ramsey; cover design by Lena DeYoung.

Print ISBN-13: 978-1-7343774-3-9

CONTENTS

Oh, that You would rend the heavens!
That You would come down!
That the mountains might shake at Your presence—
As fire burns brushwood,
As fire causes water to boil—
To make Your name known to Your adversaries,
That the nations may tremble at Your presence!
When You did awesome things for which we did not look,
You came down,
The mountains shook at Your presence.
For since the beginning of the world
Men have not heard nor perceived by the ear,
Nor has the eye seen any God besides You,
Who acts for the one who waits for Him.
Isaiah 64:1–4

PREFACE

I'm not sure how far you'll get in this book, but please make sure to read the final section, "Do You Really Want God to Rend the Heavens?"

The need to address revival and the vital role of the Holy Spirit is as relevant today as it has been throughout church history. My hope is that all of us, including myself, would humble ourselves and find the middle ground, the common ground.

The words *revival* and *spiritual awakening* are used interchangeably. Historically speaking, a revival is when God revives His people; whereas a spiritual awakening is when the masses are converted, but these spiritual experiences always overlap.

For added encouragement, I included links to articles, sermons, and podcasts below. For those reading the printed version of this booklet, all the links can be found on my website and/or YouTube channel. Simply search for the title you're interested in.

I also released another book simultaneously with this one, *40 Days to Reset Your Life: Applying God's Wisdom for Physical and Spiritual Renewal.* This resource is for those desiring to get back on track but don't know where to start—see the section "Other Books by Shane Idleman" for more information.

1. Rend the Heavens sermon here.
2. Here is a recent Podcast where I discussed some of the topics in this booklet.
3. *The sermon, True Revival Has A Cost,* can be viewed here.
4. Some relevant articles on the desperate need for revival:

- "Why Revival is America's Only Hope" here.
- "A Battle Cry for a Dead Church" here.
- "Will You Pay the Price for a National Awakening?" here.
- "Is the Future of America Worth Fighting for?" here.
- "Bored with God—Complacency in the Midst of Chaos" here.
- "America's Achilles' Heel: Powerless Sermons and Prayerless Churches" here.

Note: The exact source of some of the quotes is unknown, but most of them are well known and used often in Christian literature. We are also hoping to make the audible version of this book available soon.

1

OH GOD, RIP OPEN THE HEAVENS!

> Oh, that You would rend the heavens!
> That You would come down!
> That the mountains might shake at Your presence— . . .
> To make Your name known to Your adversaries,
> That the nations may tremble at Your presence!
> — Isaiah 64:1–2

ON APRIL 24TH, 2021, an Indonesian submarine sank in the southern Pacific Ocean. The news reported that the crew may have run out of oxygen and quickly sank below the *crush depth*—the pressure on the outside was greater than the strength on the inside. It is thought that it went down quickly because of an internal leaking.[1]

This parallels exactly what is happening in America today as waves of confusion and chaos overcome the masses. Many are being crushed by the external pressures of life because the strength on the inside (their relationship with God) is not greater than the pressure on the outside.

As I recently wrote, "America's stage four cancer has metastasized to the family and the church. We are more depraved than ever before."[2] And in a second article, I lamented, "America crossed a dangerous line years ago. Instead of repenting and turning back to God, we have walked further into the deep waters of ungodliness. The decadence and brutality in our streets are unparalleled in our history as despair and depression overcome our land. But, believe it or not, I am hopeful."[3]

How can I be hopeful amid such darkness and depravity? Because God is sovereign and controls the affairs of men. He often revives His people at very dark moments in history. Before an awakening broke out in Wales in 1904, for example, one observer noted, "It is ever the darkest hour before the dawn. The decay of religious faith, the deadness of the Churches, the atheism of the well-to-do, the brutality of the masses, all of these, when at their worst, herald the approach of the Revival."

Do we not see similar indicators today—dead churches, the decay of religion, the rise of rebellion and brutality? Don't give up! Instead, prepare the soil of your heart so that God can *rend the heavens* and release a spiritual downpour.

He Hears the Cries of His Children

Isaiah 64:1 indicates that desperation, along with repentance and humility, capture God's attention: "Oh, that You would rend the heavens! That You would come down! That the mountains might shake at Your presence." *Rend* means to burst, to blow out, to explode. What an awesome verse about an awesome God. Like any parent, He hears the cries of His children as they cry, "Oh God, would you rip heaven open and come down and help us? We are lost without you."

Yes, God is everywhere—what theologians refer to as *omnipresence*. So how can God come down if He is already here? The prophet is pleading for more of God's presence and for the overwhelming power of the Spirit to come upon us.

There are times when God seems distant, hearts feel dry, and evil is praised throughout the land. But when God comes down (literally, upon His people), we experience the joy of His presence—evil is overturned because praying men and women seek Him like never before.

As the old-timers used to say, "God heard our cries and showed up today." This is revival. This is God coming down! Would be to God that the nations would tremble again at His presence (Isaiah 64:1–2).

Who Can Stop God Almighty?

Think for a moment: Who can stop God almighty? Like Joshua and Caleb, we too can say, "We are well able to take the land" (see Numbers 13:30). Like David, we too can cry out, "Who is this enemy who dares to come against the living God?" (see 1 Samuel 17:26). And like the three Hebrew men in the fire, we can also declare, "My God will deliver me, but even if He doesn't, I will not bow to you" (see Daniel 3:17–18). And like Elijah who told 850 false prophets that God would answer by fire, we too can be assured of victory (see 1 Kings 18:24). God plus one is the majority!

What entity can ruin His plans? What leader can overpower Him? What government can override Him? What army can defeat Him? "What then shall we say to these things? If God is for us, who can be against us?" (Romans 8:31). Isaiah said that "even the mountains shake and tremble in His presence." He no doubt had Exodus 19 in mind when he penned those words. Mount Sinai was covered with smoke when the Lord's fire descended on it. The whole mountain trembled violently.

God often *shakes the physical* to get us to respond in the spiritual. Are you being shaken today? Is our nation being shaken? Do you see the calamity, decadence, and perversion all around you? If so, then why are so many "Christians" stagnant, inactive, and lifeless? Why are they not hosting *rend the heavens* prayer meetings and worship nights? Why aren't churches packed and adding more services to accommodate the hunger of God's people?

The need to rend the heavens has never been greater.

Never Let Go When God Shows Up

Do we really believe that all this evil will simply reverse itself? No, it's only going to get worse unless God's people pull down heaven. It's time to afflict the comfortable and comfort the afflicted. We must cry out, "Oh God, would you rip heaven open and come down?" We must wait on God and seek Him like never before, because He "acts for the one who waits for Him" (Isaiah 64:4).

This type of waiting expects something to happen and waits patiently for it. When we wait, anger doesn't influence us, impatience doesn't drive us, impulse doesn't derail us, and fear doesn't stop us. The disciples prayed in the upper room until heaven opened and the Spirit came down. The filling of the Holy Spirit forever changed them. They were hungry for more of God. Can you say the same?

Many years ago, a very old man who experienced a revival when he was younger was asked why the revival ended. His eyes were filled with holy fire when he cried, "When you lay hold of God, never, never, never let go!" Let this be a warning as well as a reminder to never let go.

When you were first born again, you had this fire, didn't you? And then life happened. Prayer and reading the Word gradually became an afterthought. Yet nationwide revival begins with personal revival—believers one by one begin to seek God again, and before long, there are family revivals and then churchwide revivals and then community revivals. Yes, it can happen, but the seeds must be planted by individual members of the body. In other words, it begins with you.

Are we welcoming this type of downpour in our churches and positioning ourselves for a downpour of God's Spirit, or are we extinguishing it because of pride, sin, doubt, and unbelief? It's time to break up our fallow ground and seek the Lord while He still may be found (Hosea 10:12). *We provide the sacrifice; He provides the fire.*

---

1. Hannah Beech, Muktita Suhartono and Dera Menra Sijabat, "Debris From Indonesian Submarine Is Found, Ending Hopes of Rescue," *The New York Times*, April 24, 2021, https://www.nytimes.com/2021/04/24/world/asia/indonesia-submarine-missing.html.
2. Shane Idleman, "Why Revival is America's Only Hope!" *Shane Idleman*, March 22, 2021, https://shaneidleman.com/2021/03/22/why-revival-is-americas-only-hope.
3. Shane Idleman, "Will You Pay the Price for a National Awakening?" *Shane Idleman*, April 8, 2021, https://shaneidleman.com/2021/04/08/will-you-pay-the-price-for-a-national-awakening.

2

PREPARING FOR THE DOWNPOUR

For thus says the High and Lofty One,
Who inhabits eternity, whose name is Holy:
"I dwell in the high and holy place,
With him who has a contrite and humble spirit,
To revive the spirit of the humble,
And to revive the heart of the contrite ones."
— Isaiah 57:15

IN THIS AMAZING passage of the book of Isaiah, it's clear that if we prepare the sacrifice of a broken and contrite heart, God will bring the fires of revival. It's a great reminder that His word always comes to pass.

From Isaiah 57, we also see that holiness plays a role in being revived. *Holiness* is desiring what God desires. God is love, but His name is holy. He is referred to as the Holy One of Israel over thirty times in the Bible. There were times when the church trembled at His word and walked in holiness. Those were, and still can be glorious times. God abides with those who have a humble spirit, and holiness is often a mark of humility.

To be clear, holiness involves salvation as well as sanctification. The only way to be declared holy before God is to repent of your sin and confess Christ as your Savior: "If you confess with your mouth the Lord Jesus and believe in your heart that God has raised Him from the dead, you will be saved" (Romans 10:9).

From there, we are called to live holy lives that honor God. Our decisions either fuel the fires of revival or quench the Spirit—we either rejoice in God and walk in His Word or grieve the Spirit by disobeying. The choice is ours.

Five Ways to Keep the Fire Burning

According to the Scriptures, there are five spiritual principles that often spark a spiritual awakening and keep it going. Prayer and fasting ignite the fire, but the following scriptural truths fan the flames:

1. *Embrace godly sorrow.* Second Corinthians 7:10 says that godly sorrow, in conjunction with repentance, leads to salvation. But it also leads to brokenness and dependence on God. When was the last time you wept over the condition of the nation as well as the condition of your heart? Brokenness breaks up the fallow ground of the heart—to "break off all your evil habits; clear your hearts of weeds,

in order that they may be prepared for the seed of right-eousness."[1]

2. *Recommit your life to God.* Zechariah 1:3 says, "Thus says the LORD of hosts: 'Return to me,' says the LORD of hosts, 'and I will return to you'." Once your focus is back on God, He begins to work in and through you.

3. *Restore what you can.* Genuine repentance always leads to restoration. Whether it's seeking forgiveness or mending broken relationships, you can never go wrong by making things right. In Isaiah 58, even their fasting was ineffective because they were harsh and self-focused. Pride never ushers in a spiritual awakening. A critical heart needs to be crushed under the power of the cross.

4. *Holiness is not a suggestion.* Second Corinthians 7:1 says that we must purify ourselves from everything that conta-minates our spirit. Romans 12:1 reminds us to present our bodies to God as living sacrifices, holy and pleasing to Him. Without holiness, no one will see revival.

5. *There must be continual hunger and thirst for God.* Matthew 5:6 tells us that only those who hunger and thirst for right-eousness will be filled. Continually seeking Him isn't optional; it's essential to spiritual awakenings. In studying past revivals, many of which were years or decades in the making, I've found that they all began after consistent and persistent seeking. The heat of revival never comes from a microwave setting.

Answer the Call to Return

Second Chronicles 16:9 says, "The eyes of the LORD run to and fro throughout the whole earth, to show Himself strong on behalf of those whose heart is loyal to Him." Will He find you seeking after Him or running in the other direction? Nothing is more painful than seeing an unbeliever on the broad road to destruction or a believer running from God. Return to Him today, and experience the flames of revival.

His call is to the prodigal—"Return to Me, and I will return to you" (Malachi 3:7).

His call is to the exhausted—"Come to Me, all you who labor and are heavy laden, and I will give you rest" (Matthew 11:28).

His call is to the fearful—"The peace of God, which surpasses all understanding, will guard your hearts and minds through Christ Jesus" (Philippians 4:7).

His call is to the barren—"He who believes in Me, as the Scripture has said, out of his heart will flow rivers of living water" (John 7:38).

His call is to the broken—"I will bind up the broken" (Ezekiel 34:16).

His call is to the sick—"I will strengthen the sick" (Ezekiel 34:16).

His call is to the lost—"I will seek what was lost and bring back what was driven away" (Ezekiel 34:16).

Even if you're not where you'd like to be, God's love and mercy is continually calling you back to Him.

---

1. Easton's Bible Dictionary, s.v. "Fallow-ground," accessed May 6, 2021, https://biblehub.com/topical/f/fallow-ground.htm.

3

DON'T EXTINGUISH THE FLAMES OF REVIVAL

I indeed baptize you with water unto repentance,
but He who is coming after me is mightier than I,
whose sandals I am not worthy to carry.
He will baptize you with the Holy Spirit and fire.
— Matthew 3:11

I TEND TO BE "SAFELY CONSERVATIVE." I use *The MacArthur Study Bible*, read Spurgeon's sermons, and enjoy commentaries from the Puritans. Most view me as calm and collected. My father was an extremely hardworking man who grew up on a farm in Oklahoma. As a result, I was raised in a tough environment where crying was not allowed and emotion—except for anger—was rarely shown.

In my younger years, I made fun of those who genuinely worshiped God. Sure, I would get emotional while watching the NFL or Mike Tyson's one-round knockouts. But in church? No way. I believed I was strong because I could bench-press over four hundred pounds, drink a twelve-pack of beer, and win most of the fights I was in. I didn't have control of my life—my life had control of me.

Sometime later, I began to thumb through the pages of my Bible. I realized just how far I had drifted from the truth. By God's grace, I put my complete trust in Christ. Joy, happiness, and peace filled my heart. From that came books, speaking engagements, radio programs, articles, and ultimately, a church. God took a small-town boy with learning and speech problems (barely graduating high school with a 1.8 GPA) and filled him with His Spirit. Over two decades later, I still remember that special day.

Although there are many times when I pray and worship even when I don't *feel* like it, I have received many subsequent fillings of the Spirit since that day. Whether it's when I'm preaching a sermon or during an early morning devotional, rivers of living water often pour into my soul. Boldness rises up, and zeal for God's house consumes me (Psalm 69:9). When I add fasting to the equation, my soul hungers even more for God.[1]

My goal in this booklet is to fan the flames of revival in your soul as well. Again, if you provide the sacrifice of a broken and contrite heart, God will provide the fire. You can be sure of that.

We Mock What We've Never Experienced

I've been disheartened over the years when people trivialize and mock deep and genuine experiences that others have had with God. Unknowingly, they are extinguishing the fire of the Spirit that they desperately need.

E. M. Bounds, famous for his books on prayer, once wrote about a devout Christian named Edward Payson. Payson fueled the fires of revival during the Second Great Awakening through his persistent intimacy with God. It was said that he wore grooves into his hardwood floor as a result of his many hours and hours praying. I found this story deeply inspiring, but a famous Bible teacher actually said he couldn't comprehend that kind of behavior.

How anyone can mock that is beyond me. When I read Edward Payson's story, I felt the complete opposite. Instead of being unable to comprehend his behavior, I was inspired by it and prayed: "Lord, please bring a downpour of Your Spirit into my dry and barren soul. Oh God, would You revive Me again so that I can rejoice in You?"

Praying fervently to experience the power of God as Payson did is not uncommon. Both early believers and persecuted Christians today would be shocked at how little we actually pray. It was said of John Hyde, who left for the mission field in 1892, that he would stay on his face before God until the answer came. John Welch, the great Scottish preacher who died in 1622, would sometimes spend four to six hours in prayer. John Fletcher, one of the leaders of the Methodist movement, stained the walls of his room with the breath of his prayers until he died in 1785.

What causes people to ridicule deep moments of prayer and worship? My assessment is jealousy. They mock what they've never experienced—the overwhelming power and presence of the Spirit. Sadly, spiritual pride often follows those skilled in the Word because "knowledge puffs up" (1 Corinthians 8:1). As a result, spiritual pride causes them to discount the experiences of others.

When confronted about their lack of Holy Spirit fire, they often snap back in anger, "But I'm standing for the truth! Doctrine! Doctrine! Doctrine!" Although I love theology and stand for it daily, we must also remember that we were created to experience God. If more men and women sought Him with all their heart and soul (according to the truth), America might actually experience another profound revival.

Straight as a Gun Barrel but Just as Empty

Several years ago, I was at a large conservative pastors' conference in Southern California. Most who were present were cessationists, so I was surprised when a man who escaped persecution in China told of how the Holy Spirit had prompted him to take another route on his bike. He barely escaped being caught by the police. We all applauded and thanked God for His guidance. But if a man from outside of their circle had given the same testimony, many would have said that he was misled and "hearing voices"—that God doesn't work that way today. Confused? So was I.

Don't misunderstand. We need sound doctrine. Our motto at Westside Christian Fellowship is "Times Change, Truth Does Not," but we also desperately need the power of the Spirit. It's possible to be "Bible taught," but not "Spirit-led"—straight as a gun barrel theologically but just as empty. "The letter kills, but the Spirit gives life" (2 Corinthians 3:6). Experiencing God doesn't invalidate theology; it confirms it.

Many pastors spend countless hours preparing sermons, purchasing thousands of dollars in sermon software, and buying myriads of commentaries and dictionaries, but the greatest preparation is in the prayer closet. *Before God uses a man greatly, He humbles him deeply.*

If you avoid emotional worship, extended prayer, times at the altar, and fasting for spiritual renewal, then you are not running on all eight *spiritual* cylinders. All these things are marks of Christians throughout the ages. As Charles Spurgeon once noted, "Nobody can do as much damage to the church of God as the man who is within its walls but not within its life." Are you alive spiritually? Are you hungry for more of God's presence? Or are you divisive and combative over this topic of the power of the Spirit? Sadly, the church splits I have witnessed (or small groups of people leaving) were mainly over this issue—rigid conservatives at odds with those who wanted to press in and experience God. How it must have grieved the heart of God.

A Baptism of Fire

How is it that so many pastors recommend Martyn Lloyd-Jones' fantastic book *Preaching and Preachers* yet conveniently avoid the last chapter, "Demonstration of the Spirit and of the Power"? Are they embarrassed that he drove this point home in the opening paragraph: "I have kept and reserved this last lecture, what is after all the greatest essential in connection with preaching, and that is the unction and the anointing of the Holy Spirit"?

Have you received this unction, this baptism of fire that John spoke of in Matthew 3:11? Are you truly desperate for more of God? A. W. Tozer insightfully said, "If the Lord's people were only half as eager to be filled with the Spirit as they are to prove that they cannot be filled, the church would be crowded out." I sincerely believe that the greatest need in the church today is to confess our sins, obey the Word, and to be filled with the Spirit.

God Put a Round in Oswald's Chamber

Oswald Chambers, regarding the time before he received a mighty downpour of the Spirit, admitted, "God used me during those years . . . but I had no conscious communion with Him. The Bible was the dullest, most uninteresting book in existence." Oswald was straight as a gun barrel but just as empty. A few years later he wrote, "If the four previous years had been hell on earth, these five years have truly been heaven on earth. Glory be to God, the last aching abyss of the human heart is filled to overflowing with the love of God." God put a round in Oswald's chamber and pulled the trigger. Heaven was rent; the downpour came to his parched soul.

Now, the decision is yours. Don't extinguish the flames of revival by mocking the work of the Spirit. Fully surrender your life to Him today. Christian history records countless testimonies of those who received a mighty filling of the Spirit years after conversion. The Holy Spirit in (*en*) you is not the same as the Holy Spirit upon (*epi*) you. These Greek prepositions make a world of difference.

Two of my favorite books on this topic are *Deeper Experiences of Famous Christians* by James Gilchrist Lawson, and *They Found the Secret* by Edman V. Raymond. My article "America's Achilles' Heel: Powerless Sermons and Prayerless Churches" also speaks to this important issue.[2]

Don't Handcuff My Emotions

Sadly, many conservatives also chastise emotional and extended worship, and avoid it like a plague. To them, fasting is outdated, lengthy worship is brainwashing, and weeping at the altar is too emotional. Is it wrong when prodigals come home and can't contain their emotions? Should we be embarrassed when addicts are weeping because the Savior set them free at the altar? When was the last time you wept over the condition of our churches, families, and nation? If you never have, then you fill in the blank.

Let me be brutally honest: many who show contempt for profoundly deep and moving experiences with God have never experienced them for themselves. If they avoid prayer meetings, complain about extended and emotional worship, never miss a meal for God, are unaffected by the depravity around them, and are too mature to go to the altar, are these people truly filled with God's Spirit? They love to read the Bible, but they don't want the Bible reading them. Granted, there are seasons when we aren't involved in a lot of things, but excuses should not hide our lack of hunger for God.

Do we really believe Jesus would tell us to sit down and be quiet during worship? Would He want us standing like dead men in a cemetery? Not a chance! Our hearts should be deeply engaged during worship. Jesus may rebuke silly trends and sappy worship songs with no theological bearing, but would He handcuff our emotions? I don't think so. Granted, I am not talking about becoming emotional for the sake of emotions—we can't fake a move of the Spirit. But there should be a yearning and a desire to worship God reflected in our actions. If you disagree, you'd be hard-pressed to find any Scriptures to support your view.

How to Prevent Deception

Emotions can be deceptive, so we must be careful (more on this later). George D. Watson notes, "The true saints of

God . . . have in all generations had to walk between the two extremes of cold formality on the one side, and wild, ranting fanaticism on the other. Dead formality and the false fire of fanaticism are both Satan's counterfeits, and he does not care into which extreme the soul plunges."

On this point, D. Martyn Lloyd-Jones reminds us that "we should never interpret Scripture in the light of our experiences, but rather interpret our experiences in the penetrating light of Scripture." We can prevent deception by making truth the engine of the train and emotions the caboose. Emotions don't lead; they follow. But when God's Spirit is truly moving, our emotions will be engaged. One example of this is illustrated in the life of Griffith Jones, who preached during the Welsh revivals of the eighteenth century: "The tears [of the congregation] began to flow in streams down their cheeks. Soon, they wept openly, and cried out, 'What shall we do to be saved?'"

When our experience lines up with Scripture, the emotions that follow can be good and God-given. We are in good company—God's company.

Don't Confuse Me with the Facts

During the beginning of the lockdown in 2020, right before we reopened our church in California (as did Pastors Jack Hibbs, Rob McCoy, and John MacArthur and their churches), I preached a series on genuine revival.[3] Some people voiced concern over a guest worship leader who led worship via a video feed. I asked those with concerns four questions:

1. Were the services God-honoring?
2. Were the lyrics theologically sound?
3. Were the messages biblically accurate?
4. Could there be abundant fruit?

Not surprisingly, no one responded to my questions.

Proverbs 18:13 reminded me to reach out to this "controversial" worship leader before forming a judgment: "A foolish person answers a matter before hearing both sides" (my paraphrase).[4] Again not unexpectedly, none of the critics apologized after the interview revealed that 99 percent of the information about her wasn't true. Apparently, all of them had already made up their minds, and they didn't want to be confronted with the facts.

Granted, I share many of your concerns about some of the "weird" churches out there, but I try to draw my conclusions by going directly to the person in question (when possible). Anyone can manipulate footage and quote things out of context.

Embarrassed in the Upper Room

Although I consider myself a conservative, I often wonder how so many conservatives can quote people like George Whitefield and Jonathan Edwards but conveniently avoid the mighty, uncommon moves of the Spirit that occurred under their preaching. Is it because these things don't fit within their theological framework?

Although many powerful experiences during these spiritual awakenings parallel the books of Acts, many critics still refuse to accept them. They avoid words and phrases like *revival, moves of the Spirit,* and *the deeper life,* but these themes are used throughout the Bible. How many times did God say that He would "pour out His Spirit"? How often was the heart-cry of God's people focused on revival —"Will You not revive us again, that Your people may rejoice in You?" (Psalm 85:6). And isn't seeking God with all our heart part of the deeper life? Absolutely. The living water Jesus spoke about is not dead and stagnant.

Why would we fear encountering God in powerful and profound ways? To be stoic and stiff is fine for a graveyard but not for a dynamic worship service. I wonder if these types of people would be embarrassed if they were in the upper room when the Holy Spirit came upon the disciples on that historic day in Acts 2? I think they would.

Everything Should be Done in Order

If a pigskin can travel a hundred yards across a football field and millions get emotional, shouldn't Christians saved by the power of God get emotional when they experience Him? Sadly, 1 Corinthians 14:40 is often used as a fire extinguisher to quickly quench anything out of the ordinary: "Let all things [in the church] be done decently and in order."

Sometimes I'm accused of being "too conservative" because I want to honor this verse. I believe that a "circus" environment is not healthy or beneficial, but I also believe that a cemetery setting can be just as damaging and damning. When sinful men encounter a holy God, it's often controversial. We need shepherds who can steward the flame of revival, not snuff it out.

I will never forget many years ago when a man found his way to the altar during closing worship. He was weeping and crying out to God. I was a little nervous wondering what people were thinking. As I was praying, his friend came over and said that the man at the altar had just found his son hanging in the garage—suicide had taken his life. I immediately made my way to the altar and wept with him. I was flooded with so much emotion that I couldn't even pray. God broke me that day.

Another time when the service didn't go as expected was when I was speaking at a friend's church. The power of God was so apparent that I could barely get through my message without breaking down. When the service was over, no one left. There was a holy hush as tears were heard throughout the sanctuary. The first service ran into the second service (this happens on occasion at the church I lead as well). The parking lot was a mess, but it was a beautiful problem to have. Sometimes we're more worried about parking than we are about people.

George Whitefield, once perplexed by the emotional things taking place when he preached, asked Lady Huntingdon for advice on containing it. She said, "Oh George, leave them alone. What they are experiencing from God will do far more than you're preaching."

You'd have a better chance of damming up Niagara Falls than containing a move of God.

Bold but Not Weird

To be clear, I'm not validating weird behavior. Just because something is odd doesn't mean that it's of God. In my readings of charismatics and Calvinists, Pentecostals and Puritans, and countless biographies of leaders such as Martin Luther, John Knox, and Robert Murray M'Cheyne, it's clear to me that these leaders never encourage the hysteria or the outright weirdness we sometimes see today. The fruit of the Spirit is not weirdness; it's boldness. It doesn't promote hysteria; it promotes holiness.

Granted, there were times of strong conviction, such as when people held on to trees because they feared that they were falling into hell during Jonathan Edwards' famous sermon "Sinners in the Hands of an Angry God." And people did cry out to God and fall on the ground under the strong conviction of sin during the revivals of George Whitefield and John Wesley, but this is because sin, righteousness, and holiness were preached. The apostle Paul wrote that if an unbelieving or uninformed person entered a meeting where the Holy Spirit was moving, he would experience conviction, and "falling down on his face, he will worship God and report that God is truly among you" (1 Corinthians 14:25). True revival is emotional and unpredictable.

Again, don't misunderstand what I'm saying: theology is vital, but are theology students also encouraged to fast and pray as well as study? How often are they taught broken-ness and repentance in addition to translating the Greek language? How often are they taught the surrendered life? We can sometimes be more concerned about a master's degree than a degree from the Master.

The Forgotten God

The Holy Spirit inspired the Scriptures and empowered Jesus and the apostles. We are desperately remiss if we fail to recognize His vital role in our lives. I agree with Leonard Ravenhill, who said, "We need to close every church in the land for one Sunday and cease listening to a man so we can hear the groan of the Spirit which we in our lush pews have forgotten."

Are you truly a lover of His presence? Or have you been guilty of mocking the work of the Spirit? Take time now and humble yourself before God. I believe that a genuine spiritual awakening can take place. God will rend the heavens and fill you with His Spirit.

---

1. Paul Washer breaks down the importance of fasting in "Fasting and Weeping Paul Washer," July 24, 2020, YouTube, https://youtu.be/mrSEtvaGnPU.
2. Shane Idleman, "America's Achilles' Heel: Powerless Sermons and Prayerless Churches," April 23, 2021, *Shane Idleman*, https://shaneidle-man.com/2021/04/23/americas-achilles-heel-powerless-sermons-and-prayerless-churches.
3. You can hear the service here: Westside Christian Fellowship, "Igniting Revival—Dead Bones Come Alive," May 9, 2020, YouTube, https://youtu.be/NQDf6qjuptA.

4. You can watch the interview at "Exclusive - Shane Idleman Interviews Kim Walker Smith (Powerful and Impactful)," YouTube, November 11, 2020, https://youtu.be/KOY-5cpqzwE.

4

IF IT'S ODD, IT'S NOT NECESSARILY GOD

Beloved, do not believe every spirit, but test the spirits,
whether they are of God;
because many false prophets have gone out into the world.
— 1 John 4:1

CHRISTIANS CAN EMBRACE one of two extremes concerning the word *revival*. At one extreme are those who embrace pure emotionalism and hysteria—"If it's odd, it's God"—and all weird behavior is excused. The other extreme, that I just addressed, lacks a living, vibrant spiritual life. The church feels dead, cold, and lifeless. Talk of reviving the things of God (revival) is either dismissed or ridiculed. Both extremes can hinder the work of the Holy Spirit and genuine Christian growth.[1] In this section, I will primarily address the first extreme of hysteria and pure emotionalism.

I have viewed videos of people supposedly "getting high," "toking," and "drunk" on the Holy Ghost. This is not the same as being "filled with the Spirit" (Ephesians 5:18). I have also seen video footage of people being led around like dogs on a leash and acting like animals. Yes, I'm serious—bizarre and grossly unbiblical manifestations are not reflective of one filled with the Spirit. Those truly filled with the Spirit reflect the personality and nature of God.

I Know It Seems Bizarre, but ...

When people are questioned about extremes in this type of odd behavior, they cannot give any answers from Scripture. Common responses are "I know it seems bizarre, but ..." or "I know it's weird, but ..." or "You're quenching and grieving the Spirit by not being open." These are not biblically sound responses to such bizarre manifestations. The Holy Spirit is not quenched when we honor God's Word and "test the spirits, whether they are of God" (1 John 4:1). He is quenched and grieved when we do not test and discern—when we allow the Holy Spirit to be misrepresented.

The apostle Paul said that we are to judge, or discern, all things (1 Corinthians 2:15). Someone truly filled with the Spirit, although bold, is often not bizarre. Sadly, Scripture is often used in an attempt to support very odd behavior. For example, Acts 2:15 states, "For these are not drunk, as you suppose, since it is only the third hour of the day," and John 18:6 records that men "drew back and fell to the ground" when Jesus surrendered Himself shortly before

His death. These Scriptures when used to validate wild, ranting fanaticism are incorrect and misleading. Granted, we cannot dismiss the truly miraculous works of God that happen daily, nor can we minimize the incredible power of God to radically change lives through the power of the Spirit. However, in our zeal and excitement, we often minimize the need for discernment.

Sincere but Wrong

A discerning person considers supernatural experiences in light of God's Word, His nature, and His character. They ask, "Is there genuine fruit?" In other words, does the experience align with God's Word? Is the fruit of the Spirit found in Galatians 5:22–23 present: love, joy, peace, long-suffering, kindness, goodness, faithfulness, gentleness, and self-control? A true, genuine experience with the Holy Spirit will produce godly fruit and obedience to God. It seeks to promote those things that are pure and righteous.

A word of caution here. Even those in the New Age movement experience powerful feelings of love and euphoria, but it doesn't draw them closer to Christ or lead to repentance or surrender to the true God. Although sincere, we can be sincerely wrong and seriously misled. Having an experience or being enlightened can create "feel-good" emotions, but it does not necessarily mean it is of God.

Even though there is flexibility and freedom, our experiences must align with the Scriptures and the character of God. As previously stated by Lloyd-Jones, "We should not interpret Scripture in the light of our experiences, but rather, interpret our experiences in the penetrating light of Scripture."

Do Not Touch My Anointed Ones

Feelings can be good and God-given; however, we cannot forget the prophet Jeremiah's words, "The heart is deceitful above all things, and desperately wicked; who can know it?" (17:9). Profoundly moving experiences do stir emotions, and they may "feel" right, but emotions are primarily a vehicle for expression, not a gauge for truth.

Sadly, some of the disturbing behavior mentioned earlier has been excused, and some of the leaders of these movements are rarely challenged. They can divorce their spouses and remain in leadership using 1 Chronicles 16:22 as a proof text, "Do not touch My anointed ones, and do My prophets no harm." This is an abuse of grace at the highest level and a twisting of Scripture. We should forgive, but reinstatement raises several questions.

In our zeal to defend the Holy Spirit, we sometimes run the risk of defending wrong behavior. One can rise to the top because of ability but plummet to the bottom because he or she lacks spiritual character. Throughout the Old Testament, God gave people the opportunity to be leaders, but it was their character and their humility, not their position, that determined their outcome.

To counter this criticism, some of the followers of this movement say that those who oppose them will suffer the judgment of God when in reality, it is those who refuse

God's offer of salvation who will suffer judgment. A person is not judged for seeking discernment—they are judged for rejecting the truth (see Romans 1:18).

What You Seek You Find

Although some well-intentioned Christians are anxious to hear from God, many seek signs and wonders rather than seeking Him. We can become unstable, confused, and deceived when spirituality hinges only on signs, wonders, and manifestations. Instead, "seek first the kingdom of God and His righteousness" and everything else will fall in place (Matthew 6:33).

Please understand, it's not my intention to paint "experience-oriented" movements with a broad brush—God wants us to experience Him. The presence and the power of the Holy Spirit can provoke overwhelming feelings, and rightly so. When truth penetrates the heart, excitement, passion, and enthusiasm often follow. As stated earlier, these emotions can be good and God-given. My goal is not to limit the gifts, power, and presence of the Spirit but to seek balance and discernment.

One of the reasons people embrace unbiblical experiences is because they are not in the Word seeking balance, confirmation, and discernment. Simply stated, if we are not in the Word, the Word will not be in us. We can easily be deceived. Searching for spiritual fulfillment isn't wrong, but where we search can be. Spiritual hunger is good, yet we can be so hungry spiritually that we'll consume anything. Eagerness to consume can lead to experience-oriented movements with no scriptural basis, especially when we begin to look to experiences to validate truth. God is working whether we "feel" something or not.

Toking the Holy Ghost

Some of the events where oddities occur can feed sinful desires rather than challenge them. Granted, some people who attend these events are truly seeking God. I'm not minimizing that; I applaud them for seeking, but the "signs and wonders" gospel is not the real gospel. Nor is the "prosperity gospel" the real gospel. God may prosper us, and miracles do happen, but these are secondary—Christ is primary.

Many godly people do not experience great prosperity, which can be a blessing because riches often draw us away from God. The greatest miracle is that God saved us and now calls us to help others. Granted, Christians can look odd to the culture, and God is not predictable, but this is not what I'm referring to. Instead, I'm referring to bizarre occurrences such as people appearing drunk at the pulpit, "toking" the Holy Ghost, acting like animals, and screaming as if they were on fire. Can we honestly believe that Jesus, Peter, and Paul would endorse or, worse, partake, in such weird behavior?

The apostle Paul often warned against confusing and immature behavior that compromises the gospel. False-hood and confusion often go hand-in-hand. Paul often corrected errors in his epistles, and in 1 Corinthians 14:40 he concludes, "Let all things be done decently and in order." Rather than quenching and grieving the Spirit, Paul is pleading for sound action, decency, and order within the church when possible (as the standard). According to 1 Timothy 3:14–15, the church is to be "the pillar and ground of the truth."

Being Controversial Isn't Necessarily Wrong

There are incidences of odd behavior in the Bible, such as the man from the country of the Gadarenes who was possessed, but after He met Jesus, he was "sitting at the feet of Jesus, clothed and in his right mind" (Luke 8:35). We also have an account of a man who brought his possessed son to Jesus: "And as he was still coming, the demon threw him down and convulsed him. Then Jesus rebuked the unclean spirit, healed the child, and gave him back to his father" (Luke 9:42). In these cases, very odd behavior is the result of people needing Christ. His presence and deliverance bring peace and order.

As a student of revivals, I understand that being "controversial" isn't necessarily a bad thing. Again, God is not predictable, and odd things can happen when a sinful person is overcome by the power of God.

As I read *The Journals of George Whitefield*, the Welsh Revivals, and the first-hand accounts of the First Great Awakening in America, I found that Pastor Jonathan Edward's words were true. He observed that the work of the Holy Spirit would be evident because it would:

1. elevate the truth,

2. exalt Christ,

3. oppose Satan,

4. point people to the Scriptures, and

5. result in love for God and others.

The focus of Edwards and many more were on preaching the totality of God's Word, calling out sin, and correcting error—holiness, not hysteria, was sought. The result was genuine fruit, not ungodly fanaticism.

Not Everything Done in God's Name Bears His Approval

Some suggest that today's battle is not so much against liberals in the church but against those who are "not open" to new prophecies and visions—those who "religiously hold to the written Word alone."

This statement concerns me because it can be used to promote anything done in the name of the Lord. Granted, Acts 2:17 is relevant for us today, "And it shall come to pass in the last days, says God, that I will pour out of My Spirit on all flesh; your sons and your daughters shall prophesy, your young men shall see visions, your old men shall dream dreams." But this Scripture is balanced by 1 John 4:1, "Beloved, do not believe every spirit, but test the spirits, whether they are of God; because many false prophets have gone out into the world." Not everything done in God's name bears His approval.

Even a Broken Clock Is Right Twice a Day

A "prophet," as mentioned in the Bible, can be anyone in a position of spiritual authority or claiming to be. They are not to be elevated or idolized. We follow Christ, not men. False teachers aren't ostentatiously dressed in red, armed with pitchforks. They often look credible and talk convincingly; however, they bring destructive teachings into the church. They tend to avoid difficult truths such as sin, judgment, and repentance, and focus on what people want to hear rather than what they need to hear. False teachers provide layers of truth mixed with error, but even a broken clock is right twice a day.

Today, when the truth of God's Word is spoken, people are often offended because they've been conditioned to hear feel-good messages that do little in calling out sin. As a result, churches are filled with people whose lifestyles reflect little change. William Still said it well, "Many, who for the first time come under the sound of Holy Ghost preaching, are mortally offended . . . because they have never been exposed to the white light of the Spirit."

Wisdom requires that we examine what is being sought and taught—that is, what's the focus? Repentance, holiness, obedience, and purity should be primary rather than boasting, blessings, abundance, and prosperity.

Jesus warns, "Beware of false prophets, who come to you in sheep's clothing, but inwardly they are ravenous wolves" (Matthew 7:15). There are false teachers within the church. We are encouraged to pray for wisdom and discernment.

"Words from the Lord" should not supersede the Bible but, instead, confirm it. "Prophecy involves not authoritative Bible teaching, and not speaking words of God which are equal to Scripture, but rather reporting something which God spontaneously brings to mind."

We hold religiously to the written Word because it is our guide—to test what is being said: "The spirits of the prophets are subject to the prophets" (1 Corinthians 14:32). The speaker should be careful since his words must be under, or subject to, God's Word. If those who look to the Word are accused of quenching and grieving the Spirit, we are reminded that Jesus used the Word of God for finality, discernment, and power.

But What if a Prophet Is Wrong?

Can a person have the gift of prophecy yet still make a mistake, in which case a "contrite" apology is required? What are we to say to this? The prophecy fiasco during the 2020 election is one such example. But I don't think we can make a blanket statement, nor should we let opinions sway our thinking.

For example, I know very godly people with the gift of prophecy. They've been so accurate that only God could have revealed the information they conveyed. But there have been a few times where these same people told me things that didn't come to pass. So, are they false prophets?

In the Bible, it's crystal clear that false prophets intentionally deceive people. Jude 4 says that "certain people have crept in unnoticed who long ago were designated for this condemnation, ungodly people, who pervert the grace of our God into sensuality and deny our only Master and Lord, Jesus Christ" (ESV). The people mentioned above, however, love the Lord, but they allow emotion and personal desire to lead their words. Some become overconfident because of past accuracy.

I don't consider these people false prophets. Their mistake was that they didn't take their "word" to the Lord and ask for confirmation. They *reacted* on impulse rather than *receive* a true burden from the Lord, much like the prophet Nathan who told King David, "Go, do all that is in your heart, for the Lord is with you" (2 Samuel 7:3). It was a good idea for David to build the temple, but it was not a God idea. God corrected Nathan and told him that David was not to build a house for Him.

A false proclaimer of God's truth is much different than godly Miss Marth (not her real name) who loves the Lord and has the gift of prophecy but missed it because of her desire for godly leadership (as in the case of Trump's reelection, for example). Granted, if Miss Marth keeps "missing it," we may have a problem on our hands—but not necessarily a false prophet. In this case, she needs to take a season and not exercise this gift and, instead, seek God for wisdom and discernment. I would also add that people should not be quick to exercise this gift. It should be a burden God puts on you that can be tested and weighed by others.

An Example of the Gift of Prophecy

A true prophetic word is specific and often speaks to a particular issue in your life. It will always align with Scripture and God's wisdom and is never to take the place of God's Word.

I will never forget a night in 2003 when my wife and I were visiting a church. I was digging ditches and working hard in the construction industry after coming back to the Lord a few years prior. Each day when I studied God's Word, I kept sensing powerful, bold messages rising up in my spirit. At one point, I even told my wife, "These messages are very bold. People are going to think I'm arrogant if I say these things." I knew God was calling me to preach, but I kept backing down because of what I mentioned to my wife. It was a crucial turning point—would I become a preacher or a motivational speaker?

Approximately two hundred people were present at the service. The man who was the guest speaker that night completely spoke to this issue, saying, "God is giving you boldness; it's not arrogance" (hear it here.) It was life-changing and just what I needed in order to move forward. It has motivated me countless times to preach boldly in the face of adversity. That's why it's called a *gift*. The Spirit helps us discern God's will and confirm His calling on our life.

Another time, years later, was when I was really struggling with saying some hard things that morning. I was at early morning worship at 6 a.m., but I was really struggling. As I prayed, I kept telling God that I cannot say those things because I don't know if it's Him or me. I need confirmation. Within a minute, a very godly older woman named Maryland was kneeling at the altar. She got up and walked straight to me and said, "Say everything that God puts on your heart—don't hold back anything."

Are these incidents—and many more—simply coincidence? Not a chance.

A Final Word to Those Who Mislead

A false prophet intentionally misleads people by influencing them to act in a way contrary to God's Word. They also don't apologize when wrong. Granted, even false prophets sometimes apologize to mask their mistake, but the apology is more of an excuse ("This is what I *really* meant"). False prophets are often flamboyant but lack godly character. They usually include the title of *prophet* or *apostle* on their business card. They are wolves in sheep's clothing, and they often focus on making money.

Have you been manipulating, conjuring, or falsely misrepresenting the work of the Spirit? Don't live your life with a question mark here. Those who are truly saved want to protect and honor the work of the Spirit. Don't waste another minute living like this. Take time now and repent. God will rend the heavens and fill you with His Spirit.[2]

1. Although much of the content here is new, I also include excerpts from my books *Desperate for More of God* and *Answers for a Confused Church.*

2. For more on the topic, see "The Battle for Truth—7 Unmistakable Traits of False Prophets," *Shane Idleman,* July 13, 2020, https://shaneidleman.com/2020/07/13/the-battle-for-truth-7-unmistakable-traits-of-false-prophets; and "Prophetic Standards Statement" Prophetic Standards, accessed May 6, 2021, http://propheticstandards.com. After many failed prophecies about the reelection of President Trump, a statement was released in 2021 that discussed the legitimate role of prophecy in the church. Although I don't agree with every point, the statement lays it out well.

REVIVAL WILL COST YOU

Jesus said to them, "Can the friends of the bridegroom
mourn as long as the bridegroom is with them?
But the days will come when the bridegroom
will be taken away from them, and then they will fast.
— Matthew 9:15

DECADES AGO, Gordon Cove challenged readers when he wrote, "You have not sought the Lord with 'your whole heart' until you have tried a protracted season of prayer and fasting." Could a lack of prayer and fasting be one of the hindrances to a spiritual awakening? Absolutely! Desperate times call for desperate measures. A full stomach makes seeking God difficult, prayer hard, and worship challenging.

Cove continues, "In many cases, where fasting has been added to the prayers, along with deep consecration and weeping before God, the answer has miraculously come to hand." Fasting doesn't twist God's arm, but it does bend my knee. Fasting isn't a work; it's exchanging one appetite for a greater one.

The Spark that Ignites the Flame

My goal isn't to overemphasize fasting, but it's clear that fasting has fallen by the wayside and King Stomach is still on the throne. In reading about the spiritual renewals under the preaching of John Wycliffe, William Tyndale, Duncan Campbell, Evan Roberts, and the Puritans, as well as those in the First and Second Great Awakenings, I have found that, along with keeping the Word of God front and center, intense prayer and vigorous fasting were the sparks that ignited the flame. God heard the cry of His children. Fasting is more about desperation than discipline.

Granted, in the same way that we cannot produce a field of corn by making it rain, a spiritual awakening cannot be orchestrated. It's God's work alone, but we can prepare the soil of our heart by fully surrendering our lives. God revives those who submit themselves to Him with open and empty hands (Isaiah 57:15).

Jesus said that when He is taken away, His disciples would fast—notice He said, "when you fast," not "if you fast" (Matthew 9:15; see also 6:16). The excuses range from "It's not for us today" and the infamous "I'm just not convicted about fasting" to my personal favorite: "Fasting is legalistic." Leonard Ravenhill was famous for saying, "The things in the Bible that we don't like we call legalism," and that definitely applies to excuses about fasting.

A. W. Pink, in *Gleanings from Joshua*, said, "It would indeed be strange if we apprehended how that on the one hand Canaan was a free gift unto Israel, which they entered by grace alone; and on the other, that they had to fight for every inch of it!" Although we are totally dependent on God, a spiritual awakening will not come without a fight.

In the book of Joel, the people's provisions had dried up and withered away. They were desperate and despondent, but God didn't give up on them. To show the magnitude of their sin and the need for humility, God told Joel to consecrate a fast and cry out to Him. Crying out, fasting, and repentance were the sparks that ignited the flame (Joel 1:4–14; 2:12–17).[1]

So Close, Yet So Far

Many people *say* that they desire a spiritual awakening, but when it actually happens, they are often the first to criticize it. A spiritual awakening, especially in a corporate setting, deeply affects emotions because sin is brought to the surface and spiritual deficiencies are brutally exposed. Unless a person's heart is tender and pliable, they don't like those things happening to them. As a result, they develop a hard heart to deep movements of the Spirit. If I had a dollar for everyone who left the church because worship was too emotional and convicting, I'd have a nice slush fund.

I'm shooting you straight: the biggest critics of this book will be those who need to hear it the most. They like the section on false prophets: "Go get them, Shane!" But they will tune out the rest because they're not in tune with the Spirit. They prefer to be stoic, dispassionate, and unmoved. Because the doctrine of the Holy Spirit exposes their complacency and lack of spiritual fervor and fire, they prefer to only talk about the Father, the Son, and the Holy Word. How truly sad it is—like a man dying of thirst in a boat on a beautiful lake but too scared to jump in. They are barren, dry, and thirsty yet so close to living water.

Do You Really Want God to Rend the Heavens?

I've released these closing paragraphs a few times over the years. The relevance is so important that I'd like to share it with those who may have never read it:

Nearly a decade ago, I prayed, "Lord, bring revival to the churches," but I was not ready for the response that followed. After I prayed, it was almost as if God was saying,

You don't want revival—it will ruin your schedule, your dignity, your image, and your reputation as a person who is 'well balanced.' Men will weep throughout the congregation. Women will wail because of the travail of their own souls. Young adults will cry like children at the magnitude of their sin. With the strength of My presence, the worship team will cease playing. Time will seem to stand still. You won't be able to preach because of the emotions flooding your own soul. You'll struggle to find words but only find tears. Even the most dignified and reserved among you will be broken and humbled as little children. The proud and self-righteous will not be able to stand in My presence. The doubter and unbeliever will either run for fear or fall on their knees and worship Me—there can be no middle ground. The church will never be the same again.

Do you truly want revival? It will cost you.[2] National revival begins with personal revival. We must look in the mirror, repent, and turn completely toward God. Take time now, and fully embrace His promises: "Return to Me, and I will return to you. If you seek Me, you will find Me. If you hunger, you will be filled. If you thirst, you will be satisfied."[3]

We think that we are waiting on God, but often, He is waiting on us.[4]

---

1. This section was excerpted from my article "Will You Pay the Price for a National Awakening?" *Shane Idleman*, April 8, 2021, https://shaneidleman.com/2021/04/08/will-you-pay-the-price-for-a-national-awakening.
2. Watch the sermon "True Revival Has a Cost" October 10, 2018, YouTube, https://youtu.be/zYfN3jHqek4.
3. See Joel 2:12; Jeremiah 29:13; Matthew 5:6; John 4:14.
4. If you've wandered from God and need encouragement, then listen to this brief sermon clip: https://www.youtube.com/watch?v=Cf8M-SnodvGs

OTHER BOOKS BY SHANE IDLEMAN

1. *40 Days to Reset Your Life:* Whether it's a global reset, a financial reset, or a health reset, it's clear that we are intrigued with starting over. America is dying spiritually. Just look at the media choices that fill our homes, the sexual perversion that is running rampant, the disdain for God, and the catastrophic legislation that is governing our nation. Do we really think that we can flood our homes with sin, satisfy the gods of alcohol, lust, and addiction, mock God's Word, and expect His blessings? No . . . We need a spiritual reset. Although this book is focused primarily on spiritual health, we shouldn't overlook physical health. Many people spend the last decade or two of their lives dying rather than living—confined to homes, frequenting hospitals, and depending on others. Sooner or later, poor health choices catch up to us. It's time for a physical reset as well.

2. *Feasting and Fasting:* When the body rests and is allowed to heal, many call the results *miraculous*, but this is just how God created us. Fasting not only creates an environment of health and healing, but more importantly, it facilitates spiritual growth. There are also free download links available on some of the platforms.

3. *HELP! I'm Addicted:* We are at the crossroads: Opioid and alcohol abuse are leaving a path of

destruction in their wake. Pornography is desecrating families. Obesity is skyrocketing and plaguing millions—it has even reached epidemic levels in children. Cancer and heart disease are the number one killers in America. And on and on it goes from nicotine to caffeine to food—as a society, we are out of control. But are there answers? Yes, there are, if we once again set our sites on God's truth.

4. *If My People:* Hopeless headlines dominate the news cycle, and it's called *psychological warfare,* and the goal is to elevate stress to the point of exhaustion and then fuel fear so that people lose hope. To win this battle (the battle of the mind), Christians must saturate their minds in the Word and ways of God. The new book by Pastor Shane, *If My People,* is a cry for us to turn back to God, to seek His face, and to receive the blessings He promises to those who will humble themselves.

5. *Desperate for More of God:* One of the greatest joys associated with pastoring is seeing others filled with the Spirit of God—"You will seek me and find me when you seek me with all your heart" (Jeremiah 29:13). This is what I'm seeking to do in this book—to fan the flames of passion toward God.

6. *One Nation Above God:* "What America is and has been was the result of previous generations; everything she will become depends on the rising generation. Shane fully understands this and has provided our next generation of leaders with an

understanding of the principles that will keep America great. This book can help secure America's future as 'one nation under God.' " — David Barton, President and Founder, WallBuilders, Aledo, Texas.

7. *Answers for a Confused Church:* "Shane Idleman rings a clarion bell for the church today, calling it to its primary duty, to proclaim the truth in the power of the Holy Spirit. The church is not called to make the Gospel acceptable but to make it clear. That is preaching the truth. Shane gives a stark reminder to the Emergent Church Movement." Alex Montoya Associate Professor of Pastoral Ministries, The Master's Seminary in Sun Valley, California.

8. *What Works for Men:* Whether single, married, or divorced, all of us have made mistakes and have probably fallen short of our hopes and expectations. God's Word provides direction and encouragement through challenges and tough decisions; thus, a large portion of *What Works for Men* draws from biblical principles and is intended to inspire and motivate.

9. *What Works for Young Adults:* "Sit down, buckle up, and hold on! This is one of the best resources for young adults in the publishing industry today." Tim Wildmon, American Family Association.

10. *What Works for Singles:* This resource will help those who are single and looking to marry in the

future as well as those who have experienced the painful realities of divorce.

II. ***What Works When "Diet's" Don't:*** Learn what works, what doesn't, and why when it comes to losing weight and keeping it off. This book approaches weight loss from a biblical perspective and offers hope and encouragement. Diets don't work, but lifestyle changes do.